What Are Taylor Swift's Eras?

by Niki Catherine

illustrated by Laurie A. Conley

Penguin Workshop

For my fellow Swifties.
And thank you to Taylor Swift, for writing the
soundtrack to every chapter of our lives—NC

PENGUIN WORKSHOP
An imprint of Penguin Random House LLC
1745 Broadway, New York, New York 10019

First published in the United States of America by Penguin Workshop,
an imprint of Penguin Random House LLC, 2025

Visit us online at penguinrandomhouse.com.

Library of Congress Cataloging-in-Publication Data is available.

Printed in the United States of America

ISBN 9798217050390 (paperback)   10 9 8 7 6 5 4 3 2 1 CJKW
ISBN 9798217050406 (library binding)   10 9 8 7 6 5 4 3 2 1 CJKW

Contents

What Are Taylor Swift's Eras?

On May 9, 2024, Taylor Swift resumed the Eras Tour in Paris, France, after a two-month break. But Taylor wasn't just resting between shows . . . she was working hard. Three weeks before the Paris show, she had released a double album, *The Tortured Poets Department* and *The Tortured Poets Department: The Anthology*, containing a total of thirty-one new songs. Throughout the first shows of her massive tour across North and South America, the set list had remained largely unchanged with a few exceptions. But as the countdown clock began that night in Paris, fans were curious if she'd be adding a new set for the new album or if things would stay the same. After all, the Eras Tour was so successful already. Taylor could leave it as it had been, and everyone would still be happy with the spectacular three-hour show she had originally created.

Throughout the show, fans—also known as "Swifties"—noticed some changes. The order had been rearranged, songs had been cut, and Taylor wore several new costumes. Did this mean a new section of the show would be added for *The Tortured Poets Department?*

The *1989* era came to an end. The audience whispered to one another, eager to see what would come next. Normally at this point in the show, Taylor had a costume change, with the help of her dancers, before she performed the surprise songs. But this time, the stage went totally dark. A video played of white papers fluttering down and a long desert road. The dancers emerged in new white costumes. Finally, Taylor rose from below the stage in a beautiful white gown.

Fans cheered and screamed. The *Tortured Poets Department* era had begun.

Defined as a distinct period of time with particular features or characteristics, an era can describe the fashion of a period, a political figure or event, or even the technology of a time. But for Taylor Swift, an era describes the lifespan of an album. Each of Taylor's albums represents a unique musical era in her career, characterized by specific colors, fashion, images, themes, music genres, and more.

At the start of the show in Paris, Taylor told the crowd, "So you and I? We're about to go on a grand adventure together. And that adventure is going to span eighteen years of music and we're going to be doing this one era at a time. How does that sound to you, Paris?"

As Taylor herself would say: *Are you ready for it?*

CHAPTER 1
The *Taylor Swift* Era

Before moving to Nashville in 2003, Taylor signed a deal with RCA Records, one of the biggest record companies in the music industry. But after a year, they didn't think Taylor would be ready for an album until she was eighteen years old. That was four years away for the fourteen-year-old! So instead of renewing her deal, Taylor went back to playing her music around Nashville.

Taylor Swift, 2003

In 2004, she finally got the attention of music executive Scott Borchetta while playing a show at the Bluebird Cafe. He wanted to offer her a deal with his new record company, Big Machine Records.

Her self-titled debut album was released on October 24, 2006. *Taylor Swift* was a country album, with country music elements like a bit of twang in her vocals and featured instruments like fiddles and banjos. While Taylor didn't have a tour of her own during this time, she did get the opportunity to tour  with many top country acts such as Rascal Flatts, Brad Paisley, and Tim McGraw and Faith Hill. She was their "opener," which means she performed for the audience before the country stars began their shows.

In this era, Taylor celebrated being the typical American teenage girl. She was only sixteen years old, still in high school, and she just wanted the opportunity to write and sing her songs. Her first single, "Tim McGraw," was released on June 19, 2006, and it took radio stations by storm, reaching number six on the Hot Country Songs chart. With her first single also came her first music video. It highlighted a summer in the

countryside, with pickup trucks and open fields. Other singles included "Our Song," "Teardrops on My Guitar," and "Should've Said No."

The teal-blue and green album cover was bright and beautiful, with butterflies and Taylor front and center. Along with the country music genre, Taylor embraced some elements of country style as well and often wore cowboy boots and flowy sundresses during this time. Objects and settings that represent this era include small hometowns, grassy fields, cowboy boots, white dresses, flowers, and guitars. This era is youthful and relatable, and it is considered very "girl next door." "Girl next door" is a phrase used to describe someone as a likable girl who is approachable and sweet.

The debut album received positive reviews and even earned Taylor award nominations like Top New Female Vocalist of the Year at the

2006 Academy of Country Music Awards and a nomination for Best New Artist at the 2008 Grammy Awards. Though she didn't win her first Grammy with this album, it was very impressive to be nominated at such a young age.

CHAPTER 2
The *Fearless* Era

Taylor's second studio album, *Fearless*, was released on November 11, 2008. She was eighteen at the time. *Fearless* was about experiencing high school and how Taylor had big feelings and big dreams. The album was mostly country, but it sounded a bit pop as well. Country instruments

like banjos, fiddles, and acoustic guitars were combined with electric guitars and strings that were more common in pop music.

The title *Fearless* was meant to encourage listeners to embrace love and life by doing the things that scare them.

She came up with the idea for the album after writing the first song, "Fearless," about a first date. Even though she was still quite young, Taylor's writing and storytelling were authentic and personal, and listeners of all ages related to her music.

After *Fearless* came Taylor's first tour of her own, and her fame continued to grow. With sparkling fringe dresses and princess ball gowns, this era's fashion was very different from the one before.

She stayed true to her country roots, but she added a bit more sparkle to them. This era also marked the first time Taylor wore red lipstick, something she'd never tried before. This would become part of her iconic look!

Thirteen!

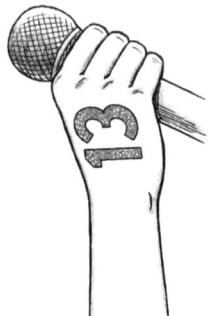

During the *Fearless* era, Taylor drew a colorful "13" on her hand for good luck. Not only is it her lucky number, it's also the date of her birthday, December 13, 1989, and many important moments in her life have happened on the thirteenth. She said in an interview with MTV that she "turned thirteen on Friday the thirteenth. My first album went gold in thirteen weeks. My first number one song had a thirteen-second intro. Every time I've won an award, I've been seated in either the thirteenth seat, the thirteenth row, the thirteenth section, or row M, which is the thirteenth letter."

Ever since the *Fearless* era, fans have taken on the tradition themselves, drawing a "13" on their hands for the Eras Tour.

Over a decade after signing her deal with Big Machine Records—the studio where Taylor had recorded her first six studio albums—the company was unexpectedly bought by a music-industry executive named Scooter Braun. He had said unkind things about Taylor in the past, leading her to worry about what would happen with her music now that he owned it. So she decided to rerecord her first six albums, add in some unreleased songs, and call them "Taylor's Version." This way, Taylor would own her songs again because she would be the owner of these brand-new

versions of them. *Fearless (Taylor's Version)* was the first Taylor's Version album. Released on April 9, 2021, it featured the original track list along with six previously unreleased tracks, which she called "From the Vault" songs. Notable duets from this album included "Breathe" featuring Colbie Caillat, "You All Over Me (From the Vault)" featuring Maren Morris, and "That's When (From the Vault)" featuring Keith Urban.

Yellow is the color fans associate with this era because both the original *Fearless* and the *Fearless (Taylor's Version)* album covers were a golden yellow shade. Each album cover also showed Taylor tossing her blond curls over her head. Some fans also say she looks like the sun, with her curls resembling its rays.

Singles like "Love Story" and "You Belong with Me" set records on both country and pop radio. The album itself became the most awarded country album of all time, winning Album of the Year at the Country Music Association Awards, the Academy of Country Music Awards, and the 2010 Grammy Awards.

CHAPTER 3
The *Speak Now* Era

Taylor's first two albums put her on the map as a songwriter. But critics said some unkind things, and several had doubts about Taylor's talent. Some thought that her songs were probably successful only because she had worked with other writers. To challenge critics, Taylor

decided that she would write her entire third album alone. This album was called *Speak Now*, and it released on October 25, 2010. Characterized by the color purple and flowery, romantic imagery, this third studio album reflected Taylor's transition from a teenager to an adult. And while *Fearless* was about doing the things that scared you, Taylor said *Speak Now* was all about finally finding the strength to say the things she had "wanted to say in the moment but couldn't."

The songs were about relationships, facing critics, fame, and growing up. The album took a closer look at the challenge of being a girl and the feelings that come with aging. *Speak Now* continued the country-pop genre with a touch of pop-rock, featuring instruments like electric guitars, drums, and violins.

Fans believe the single "Back to December" is about her relationship with actor Taylor Lautner. The song talked about asking for forgiveness from an ex-boyfriend. "Dear John" was about an unhealthy relationship between a young woman and an unkind older man. But other songs tell another story. In the lead single, "Mine," Taylor sang about finding happiness in a romance despite her fears. A fan-favorite song, "Long Live," was meant to be a love letter to her band and her fans.

Speak Now received many nominations, including Album of the Year at the Academy of Country Music Awards, the American Country Awards, and the Country Music Association Awards. It was nominated for Best Country Album at the 2012 Grammy Awards, where the single "Mean" won Best Country Solo Performance and Best Country Song. *Speak Now* also earned album wins, including Top Country

Album at the Billboard Music Awards in 2011 and Favorite Album (Country Music) at the 2011 American Music Awards.

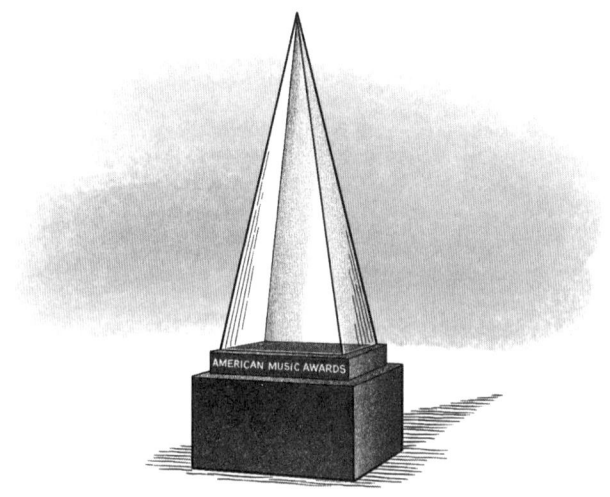

There was a *Speak Now* world tour with 111 shows. During this tour, Taylor wrote song lyrics on her arms, a tradition that fans still do today when attending her shows. She threw up heart hands (a pose in which one puts their two hands together to form the shape of a heart) to the fans from the stage. Performances were theatrical, with fireworks. Sometimes, she'd even bring out special guests. A famous item from this time was a guitar with koi fish painted on it that Taylor used on the tour. She would bring this guitar back

over ten years later during the *Midnights* era in music videos, and then onto the Eras Tour for her performances of "Long Live."

Speak Now was the first album Taylor released after leaving her teenage years, since she was twenty when it came out. Her look changed as she grew up. She would wear beautiful, romantic, sweeping gowns. She got her famous bangs at this time, but still kept her blond hair long and curly, leaning into the romantic fairy-tale imagery of the era.

At the Eras Tour, fans were surprised that the *Speak Now* album only had one song on the set list. Taylor emerged from a door on the stage amid fog before performing "Enchanted" as dancers swirled around her. For each *Speak Now* performance, she would be wearing one of many different purple ball gowns—fans never knew which she would wear on the night they went to the show.

On May 5, 2023, at an Eras Tour show in Nashville, Tennessee, purple lights illuminated a bridge in the city. Fans started buzzing. Could this be the announcement they'd all been waiting for?

Taylor approached the microphone for the surprise-song section of the show. She told the crowd she'd been planning something for them, and instead of telling them about it, she said, "I thought I would show you . . ." On the

 giant screen behind her appeared the new cover of *Speak Now (Taylor's Version)*. It featured Taylor with wavy hair in a big puffy purple gown. It was similar to the original cover, which featured Taylor in a long purple dress.

Speak Now (Taylor's Version) released on July 7, 2023, and it included "From the Vault" tracks

such as "Foolish One," "Electric Touch" featuring a band called Fall Out Boy, and "Castles Crumbling" featuring Hayley Williams. To celebrate the album release, Taylor premiered the music video for the song "I Can See You (Taylor's Version)." She brought Taylor Lautner and Joey King—the stars of the video—onto the stage. Both of the actors had been a big part of her original *Speak Now* era.

CHAPTER 4
The *Red* Era

The *Red* era is known for its autumn colors and for being a true breakup album. *Red* was released on October 22, 2012, when Taylor was twenty-two years old. It even featured a song called "22" about turning twenty-two, which fans theorize Taylor wrote because her twenty-first birthday wasn't a happy one. The name of the album came from a song of the same name that is about the feelings of being in a relationship.

The songs on *Red* dealt with themes ranging from finding and losing a new, unstable love to

Taylor's ever-rising fame and how it was both a gift and a challenge. The style continued to be a mix of country and pop, introducing elements of rock and dance music. This made it difficult for critics to properly label the album's genre. Taylor wanted the mix of music styles to represent "how messy a real breakup is."

The first song written for the album came from a tour rehearsal for *Speak Now*. Taylor stood at the microphone and made up lyrics as she played her guitar. That moment in rehearsal would later become the fan-favorite song "All Too Well."

While *Speak Now* was a way to prove her writing skills, *Red* became the album that Taylor wanted to prove her "thirst for learning" with, as she said in an interview with *Rolling Stone*.

She wanted to work with writers and producers she had never worked with before, and with these new collaborations came hits like "I Knew You Were Trouble," "Holy Ground," and the lead single "We Are Never Ever Getting Back Together." Duets on the album included "Everything Has Changed" with Ed Sheeran and "The Last Time" with Gary Lightbody.

Taylor Swift and Ed Sheeran

Red raked in many award nominations. It was nominated for Album of the Year at the Grammy Awards in 2014, the 2013 Country Music Association Awards, and the Academy of Country Music Awards. It won Favorite Country Album at the 2013 American Music Awards and Top Album and Top Country Album at the 2013 Billboard Music Awards. As had happened with her previous albums, *Red* also got a tour of its own. Taylor embarked on a world tour with eighty-six stops.

During the *Red* era, Taylor wore vintage styles including high-waisted shorts and skirts. She straightened her hair, but she continued to wear her red lip. A famous look from her "22" music video was the white T-shirt that said "Not a lot going on at the moment" and a black hat, both of which made an appearance at the Eras Tour during the *Red* section of the show.

Often, the shirts worn during this portion of the Eras Tour show would say different phrases that referenced the *Red* era or lyrics on the *Red* album.

On June 18, 2021, Taylor announced on social media that *Red (Taylor's Version)* was coming soon. It was released on November 12, 2021. It included all thirty songs Taylor had written for the original album, including "Better Man" and "Babe," which were songs she had originally created for the country bands Little Big Town and Sugarland. It would also feature a new  ten-minute version of "All Too Well." Unreleased "From the Vault" songs included "Nothing New" featuring Phoebe Bridgers, "I Bet You Think About Me" featuring Chris Stapleton, and "Run" featuring Ed Sheeran.

In her announcement, Taylor explained that "musically and lyrically, *Red* resembled a heartbroken person." She said in making the album and releasing it, "something was healed along the way."

The original album cover featured Taylor in red lipstick wearing the "22" hat and a vintage white blouse. The *Red (Taylor's Version)* cover, however, featured Taylor driving a red convertible. She wore a beige trench coat and a reddish-brown hat. The *Red* era is autumn themed—with soft sweaters, red scarves, and crunchy leaves as some of the era's symbols. Many fans associate this era with the white T-shirt and the red heart sunglasses Taylor wore in the music video for "22." Taylor also wore a circus ringleader outfit with a red jacket covered in sequins to perform at the 2012 MTV Europe Music Awards, which then became a staple on the *Red* Tour. Swifties love to re-create this costume for themselves. Fans also like to wear red scarves in reference to the song "All Too Well," in which Taylor sings about leaving behind a scarf after the end of a relationship. The color of this era is, of course, red.

All Too Well (10 Minute Version)

There was a big surprise with the release of *Red (Taylor's Version)*: Taylor had written and directed a short film for the song "All Too Well (10 Minute Version) (Taylor's Version) (From the Vault)." The film premiered on November 12, 2021, in New York City.

All Too Well: The Short Film tells the story of a bad relationship between two people, played by actors Sadie Sink and Dylan O'Brien, and the song

Sadie Sink

Dylan O'Brien

plays in the background. There is a brief section of the film that pauses the song, and the audience hears a fight between the couple. The film shows their difficult relationship and the heartbreak that follows. It won Video of the Year, Best Long-Form Video, and Best Direction at the MTV Video Music Awards in 2022, as well as Best Music Video at the 2023 Grammys and Best Short Film at the Hollywood Critics Association Awards in 2023.

CHAPTER 5
The *1989* Era

The *1989* era began with the release of the album on October 27, 2014. This album's themes included shades of blue, bright city lights,  and hints of coastal charm. Taylor left behind country and blossomed into the pop star she is today. She titled the album after the year of her birth. This was a period of big changes for the artist: She moved to New York City, cut her long blond hair short, and embraced a new sound.

During this era, Taylor's circle of friends grew. Soon, media and fans referred to them as the "squad." *1989* was about a new chapter for Taylor. It was all about enjoying life and having fun with friends, as she portrayed through two of the album's singles—"Welcome to New York" and "Shake It Off." She even featured her famous squad of friends and other women she admired in the music video for the song "Bad Blood."

Lyrically, *1989* was about new beginnings. Other singles included "Blank Space," in which Taylor sang about the judgment she experienced from the media and through gossip; "Style," which was rumored to be about her relationship with singer Harry Styles; and "Out of the Woods," which was about a stressful relationship. Some fans thought that "Out of the Woods" was about Harry Styles, too.

Harry Styles

This album was the first time Taylor collaborated with producer Jack Antonoff, a partnership that would continue for many "eras" to come. She also brought in some producers who had worked on *Red*, Max Martin and Shellback. For a song called "Clean," Taylor worked with singer Imogen Heap. The sound of the album featured 1980s-inspired synth and electropop, making songs mirror popular music from thirty years before. Many of the songs on *1989* made listeners want to dance because several of the singles were upbeat.

Even though the album was different from what her fans were used to, it quickly became a favorite and won some of the biggest music awards of that season. *1989* won Album of the Year and Best Pop Vocal Album at the 2016 Grammy Awards. It also won Album of the Year at the iHeartRadio Music Awards in 2016.

It was ranked as one of the best albums of 2014 according to various publications including *Billboard*, *Time*, and *Rolling Stone*.

The *1989* World Tour became one of the biggest concert tours of 2015, with eighty-five shows all over the world. The tour costumes included sequined jackets and colorful skirts, which were great for dancing. There were bright, colorful lights, light-up dresses, and special surprise guests at every show.

During this era, Taylor embraced her New York City life with a new city style. She wore shorter skirts, cropped shirts, and white sunglasses. To promote the album, she took photos at iconic New York City locations like the Empire State Building.

Jack Antonoff

Jack Antonoff was born on March 31, 1984, in New Jersey. He entered the music industry in 2002 with his first band, an indie rock group called Steel Train. He formed the band with a few of his friends, and Jack was the lead singer. By 2013, Steel Train had split up, and Jack was the lead guitarist in the band Fun. Jack even produced the band's first number one single, "We Are Young." During this time, he began to work on his solo music, which would later become the rock band Bleachers.

In addition to working on his own music, Jack has written and produced music for many other artists including Lorde, Lana Del Rey, the 1975, Phoebe Bridgers, Olivia Rodrigo, the Chicks, Florence + the Machine, and Taylor Swift. The first song he collaborated on with Taylor Swift was "Sweeter than Fiction."

1989 World Tour

Taylor had a lot of special guests on the *1989* World Tour. Some were musicians, models, actors, athletes, and activists. Here are some of the musicians and the songs they performed with Taylor!

Ed Sheeran: "Tenerife Sea"

Dan Reynolds of Imagine Dragons: "Radioactive"

The Weeknd: "Can't Feel My Face"

Nick Jonas: "Jealous"

Lorde: "Royals"

Little Mix: "Black Magic"

Mary J. Blige: "Family Affair"

John Legend: "All of Me"

Selena Gomez: "Good for You"

Kelsea Ballerini: "Love Me Like You Mean It"

Charli XCX: "Boom Clap"

Idina Menzel: "Let It Go" (Taylor and Idina

even dressed up as Olaf and Elsa from the Disney movie *Frozen* because the show happened on Halloween!)

On August 9, 2023, at an Eras Tour stop in Los Angeles, California, Taylor announced the release of *1989 (Taylor's Version)*. Fans had wondered if she might announce the "Taylor's Version" of this album because of some hints in Taylor's social media posts and throughout the music video of the recent single off *Speak Now (Taylor's Version)* called "I Can See You." Even the date, August 9 (8/9), lined up perfectly with the album title. The night before, on August 8, she debuted a new sparkly bodysuit for the *Midnights* portion of the show that looked very similar to one she had worn eight years before on the *1989* World Tour. The clues seemed to be there!

As Taylor performed the show that night, she introduced special new blue outfits for several of the eras (including *Speak Now* and *folklore*) leading up to the anticipated *1989* set. During that set, she had yet another new blue outfit that matched the blue colors of *1989*.

"I think instead of just telling you about it, I think I'll sort of show you—" Taylor said to the crowd as the new *1989 (Taylor's Version)* cover art appeared on the screen behind her. The cover featured  a smiling Taylor on a beach with seagulls flying around her. It was a different direction from the original cover, which was a polaroid photograph of Taylor's unsmiling red lips in the frame as she wore a sweatshirt with flying seagulls on it.

The original cover art leaned into New York City, but the "Taylor's Version" art embraced the beach. Things that fans associate with this era include Polaroid pictures, paper airplanes, New York City, the beach, and seagulls. When fans make outfits inspired by *1989*, they like to wear matching sets with a top and skirt, sometimes in colorful fringe and sequins, to match the outfits Taylor wears while performing. Many Swifties think they're fun to dance in!

CHAPTER 6
The *reputation* Era

The *reputation* era started with the disappearance of Taylor from the public eye. In the autumn of 2016, Taylor had been going through a difficult time with the media and critics due to a conflict between her and Ye, the rapper formerly known as Kanye West.

This conflict went all the way back to the *Fearless* era. When Taylor won the MTV Video Music Award for Best Female Video for "You Belong with Me" in 2009, her thank-you speech was cut short by Ye, who interrupted her speech and said that he felt someone else was more deserving of the award that year. The crowd booed, but this only made the situation worse. Taylor was incredibly embarrassed, thinking the

audience was booing her and agreeing with him. This created a years-long divide between the two artists. Later, Ye would use Taylor's name in a song, saying more unkind and inappropriate

things about her. After years of trying to keep the peace and move on, Taylor decided to tell her side of the story, so she released *reputation*.

After avoiding public appearances for about

a year, suddenly all of Taylor's social media posts were deleted across all her accounts. A video was posted of a snake. And *reputation* was released on November 10, 2017, with no other explanation.

The style of this album was a huge departure from her previous music. It explored the hip-hop and electropop genres as well as themes of anger and revenge. She brought back producers she had previously worked with like Max Martin, Shellback, and Jack Antonoff. As listeners played the album, they would be brought on the journey of Taylor's emotions as she worked on it. It started from a place of anger and ended in a place of love, celebrating a new relationship that had helped ease the pain of the situation with Ye.

Her writing was honest and angry, darker than her previous works that felt more positive and colorful. A few songs on *reputation* still had the classic softness fans loved in previous albums, such as the song "Delicate." There were—of course— still love songs.

The first single was "Look What You Made Me Do," which Taylor released with a music video. The video opened with a zombie version of the *1989*-era Taylor Swift crawling out of her grave.

Other scenes had Taylor in a bathtub of diamonds, Taylor on a throne surrounded by snakes, and Taylor singing at the top of a pile of Taylors from previous eras fighting to reach her. This was the first time Taylor used her previous "eras" in a new music video and to define her past career. Other popular singles included ". . . Ready for It?," "End Game," and "Getaway Car."

When imagining the album, Taylor said she pictured a city at night. Snakes became the symbol of the album, tying back to her conflict with Ye, during which Taylor had been called a snake in social media comments. People were using the animal as a way to call Taylor a liar and a bad person, but Taylor reclaimed that word and made it her own. She wasn't a liar, and she used *reputation* to tell her truth.

With *reputation* came a new fashion style as well. Gone were the bright colors and flowy dresses fans were used to. This album was moody, dark, and edgy. Taylor wore black bodysuits, dark lipstick, tall boots, and several pieces of snake jewelry. The album cover was black and white, featuring overlapping newspaper print and headlines over an image of Taylor with her hair slicked back. The newspaper headlines were used to call out journalists who had said hateful things about Taylor.

The era marked her first stadium tour, with a total of fifty-three shows around the world. This tour was the grandest one yet. There were flames on the stage, giant snake props, and dramatic lighting.

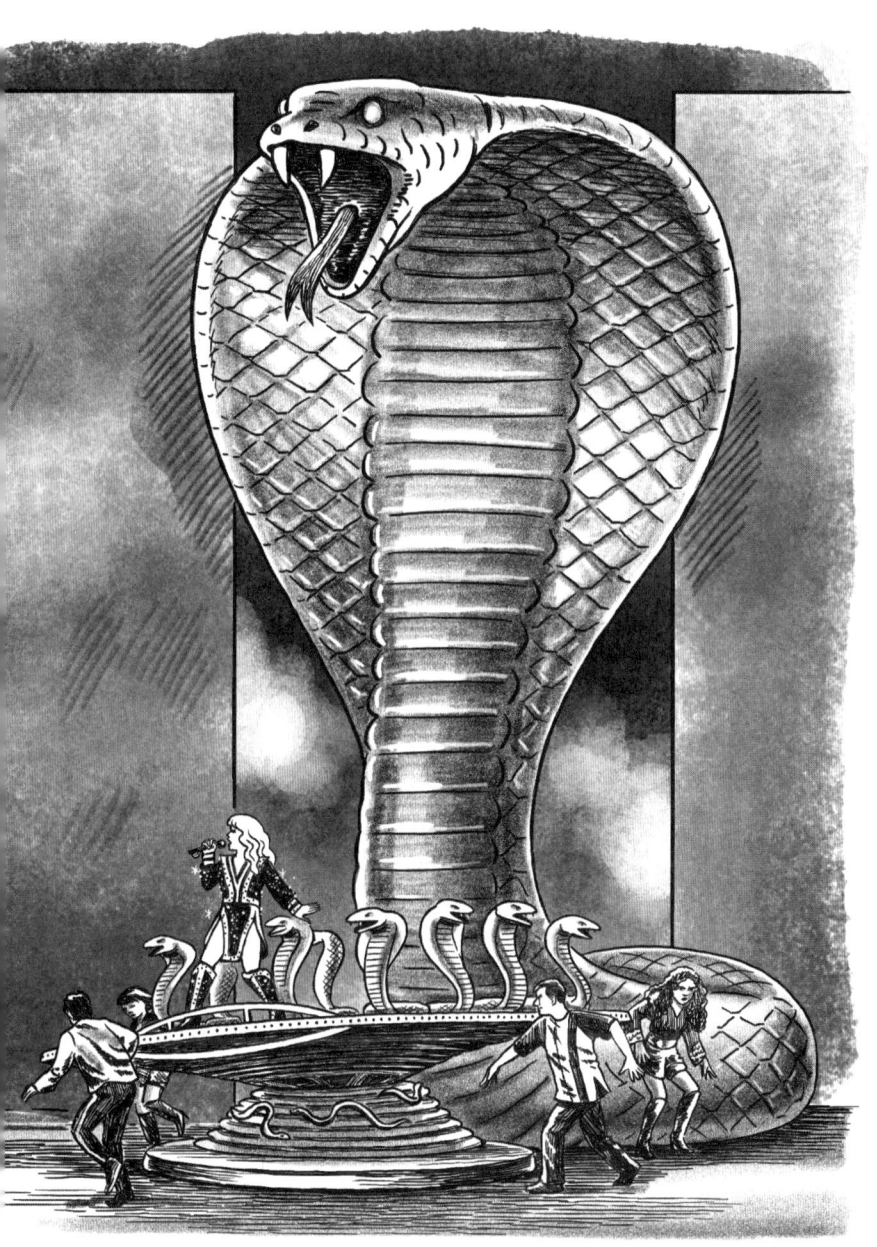

In 2018, *reputation* won Favorite Pop/Rock Album at the American Music Awards and was nominated for Best Pop Vocal Album at the Grammys. At the time, Taylor was disappointed with how the album was received, vowing to make a better album next time. But after a couple of years, music critics started to change their tune, and many now see this album as one of Taylor's best.

CHAPTER 7
The *Lover* Era

Imagine a hissing snake bursting into a hundred butterflies. That is how the transition into the *Lover* era seemed to fans. As the title hinted, this new album was "a love letter to love" and new beginnings. The snake-themed *reputation* marked the end of Taylor's contract with Big Machine Records, and—with the release of *Lover* on August 23, 2019—Taylor's partnership with Republic Records began. She was finally able to fully own her work starting with this album, and she had more artistic and creative control than ever before.

The music style was pop, but it also had elements of country and folk music. One special thing about *Lover* was that it combined many different kinds of pop music, such as electropop, bubblegum pop, and synth-pop. Taylor brought back collaborator Jack Antonoff and brought in some new producers she had never worked with before. The album's lyrics felt more personal, like love letters written by Taylor about her real life. Songs talked about the people around her and the places she lived. She left behind the anger and embraced the love she had all around her.

From friends to family to romance, this era is all about the many forms of love that humans experience. The music video for the single "You Need to Calm Down," a song in which Taylor called out hateful people and those who don't support the LGBTQIA+ community, featured many of her friends who identify as LGBTQIA+. Other singles included "Me!" (which featured

Brendon Urie) and the fan-favorite song "Cruel Summer." There was also a collaboration with country trio the Chicks, called "Soon You'll Get Better."

Aesthetically, the dreamy *Lover* era is the complete opposite of *reputation*, with pastel colors, rainbows, hearts, and butterflies. Taylor dyed the ends of her hair baby blue and wore a pink glitter heart on her face. While *reputation* is edgy and tough, Taylor described the feeling of *Lover* as "a barn wood floor and some ripped curtains flowing in the breeze, and fields of flowers."

In the way that *Red* feels like autumn, *Lover* feels like summer. The album cover featured Taylor in front of a pink-and-blue cotton candy–colored sky.

Lover hit number one on the *Billboard* 200 chart and all eighteen tracks of the album charted on the *Billboard* Hot 100. The album won Favorite Pop/Rock Album at the 2019 American Music Awards. It also won Pop Album of the Year at the iHeartRadio Music Awards and was nominated for Best Pop Vocal Album at the 2020 Grammys.

Sadly, the tour Taylor planned for this album, called Lover Fest, was canceled due to the worldwide COVID-19 pandemic. But it would get its day in the spotlight later, because Taylor chose to open the Eras Tour with *Lover*, starting with "Miss Americana and the Heartbreak Prince" and "Cruel Summer." Even though it didn't have its own tour, this era is a fan favorite because of its pastel colors and its dreamy love songs. For the Eras Tour, the *Lover* era was a very popular inspiration for fan costumes; some even re-created the colorful sequined bodysuits Taylor wore onstage. Many concert attendees wore hearts, pastels, rainbows, and butterflies to show their love for *Lover*.

CHAPTER 8
The *folklore* Era

In March 2020, a global pandemic caused most of the world to lock down. While Taylor was sheltering, she got busy writing new songs.

 On July 24, 2020, *folklore* was released, and it was a total surprise. It was Taylor's first surprise album, meaning that she announced the album on social media just twenty-four hours before it was released. Taylor said the album was something that she "poured all [her] whims, dreams, fears, and musings into." In an essay, Taylor explained that the album "started with imagery" popping

into her mind and the stories she created around those images. The album was about escaping the stress of the pandemic and instead imagining stories about a fictional, more romantic world.

The album's black-and-white cover featured Taylor lost in the woods, wearing a long coat and looking up at the trees. The world of *folklore* is rustic and cozy, full of forests, cabins, and moss-covered pianos. Taylor created a cardigan based on the first single, "cardigan," that became a beloved piece of merchandise for fans. Popular symbols for this album include that cardigan, tall trees, rustic cabins, and mirror balls, also known as "disco balls," thanks to one of the songs being titled "mirrorball."

Taylor explored an acoustic, folk sound for *folklore*, with piano, guitars, and string instrumentals. This was brand-new for her, and Taylor gained many new fans who loved this different style of music she was creating. She took on the role of storyteller in a way she hadn't before, writing songs about not only her personal life and experiences but made-up characters and stories as well. Two more singles—"exile" (which featured Bon Iver) and "betty"—were released after "cardigan."

After meeting musician and producer Aaron Dessner, Taylor asked him to cowrite some songs with her during lockdown. Dessner would send Taylor instrumentals of a song he was working on, and she would send him back lyrics. The album came together quickly. Taylor also worked with Jack Antonoff and Joe Alwyn, who was her boyfriend at the time, on some songs.

At first, Taylor wasn't sure if this was the kind of album that could be played in a stadium or even on the radio. But *folklore* debuted at number one on the *Billboard* 200 list, where it remained for eight weeks, and was the fastest-selling album of 2020. It won Album of the Year at the Grammy Awards, as well as Best Pop Album at the iHeartRadio Music Awards in 2021.

Aaron Dessner

Aaron Dessner was born on April 23, 1976, in Ohio. He is one of the founding members of the rock band the National, along with his brother, Bryce. The National has released nine albums and one of their songs was even used by former president Barack Obama in a presidential campaign video.

Following the success of their fourth album, *Boxer*, they started collaborating with other artists. Aaron has composed many film scores, including for *Cyrano* and *Big Sur*.

Aaron is also the cofounder of the duo Big Red Machine, partnering with Justin Vernon of Bon Iver. They released a self-titled album in 2018, which was recorded at Dessner's studio, where he would later record *folklore* and *evermore* with Taylor Swift. Big Red Machine's second album, *How Long Do You Think It's Gonna Last?*, was released in 2021 and featured Taylor on a song called "Renegade." Aaron has also produced and collaborated with Gracie Abrams, Ed Sheeran, Maya Hawke, and Girl in Red.

And it was a fan-favorite section of the Eras Tour, despite Taylor's initial worries. Fans who wanted to dress up like the *folklore* album at the Eras Tour would wear flowy dresses, cardigans, neutral colors, and ribbons.

CHAPTER 9
The *evermore* Era

On December 10, 2020, Taylor announced *evermore*, which she called a "sister record" to *folklore*. It was another surprise album. She  described on social media how she just couldn't stop writing and how creating this second album felt like traveling farther into the woods of *folklore* instead of turning back to leave. The sound and aesthetic of *evermore* was similar to the album that came before it. It was imaginative and emotional, with stories taking place in the woods. This album's color is rusty orange, and it feels magical, with its references to spells and witches.

Taylor continued writing lyrics in a similar style to *folklore* when she wrote *evermore*, and the music was similar, too. Writing in this style allowed her to be more creative because she could write about fictional characters instead of only being able to write about her own life.

The witchy theme of the album showed in the music video for the single "willow." It opened with Taylor in the famous folklore cardigan, following a golden thread into the Evermore Forest, where magical things took place, including Taylor and others dancing around a fire with glowing golden orbs. Other singles included "no body, no crime" (which featured the band HAIM) and "coney island" (which featured Aaron Dessner's band the National). The songs had lyrics about forbidden love, crime, forgiveness, and marriage.

HAIM

On the album cover, Taylor was in a plaid coat with her hair in a braid, facing away from the camera, looking off into a forest in front of her. Fans created outfits inspired by this era by wearing floral gowns, wool coats, plaid patterns, and turtlenecks. Popular symbols for this album include willow trees, flannel, braids, ivy, and evergreen trees.

When it released, *evermore* landed at number one on the *Billboard* 200 chart and stayed there for four weeks. It became one of the top ten bestselling albums of 2020 even though it was released within the last few weeks of the year. The album won Favorite Pop/Rock Album at the American Music Awards in 2021. It was also nominated for Album of the Year at the Grammy Awards in 2022 but did not win.

At the Eras Tour, the *evermore* section opened with a performance of "willow" featuring cloaked dancers. Tall evergreen trees emerged from the stage and a mossy piano was set to the side, awaiting Taylor's performance of fan-favorite song "champagne problems." After the show changed to include *The Tortured Poets Department*, Taylor combined the *folklore* and *evermore* sets into one big era, rearranging the songs and removing some. She called this set *folkmore*.

CHAPTER 10
The *Midnights* Era

While accepting an award for "All Too Well (10 Minute Version) (Taylor's Version) (From the Vault)" on August 28, 2022, Taylor announced her tenth studio album, *Midnights*. The songs were about real sleepless nights throughout her life.

The cover art featured Taylor in blue eyeshadow holding a flickering lighter. In the bottom left corner was the track list in the same dark blue color as the title. This made the album look similar to vinyl covers from the 1970s that had the

track lists on the front. The *Midnights* cover is moody, just like the music. The album's colors are dark blues and purples, and its music videos featured outfits, makeup, and props inspired by the 1970s, with wood walls and old telephones.

While promoting this album, Taylor wore sparkles, stars, and sequins to ring in her "Bejeweled" era ("Bejeweled" is the name of one of this album's singles). Popular symbols for this era include clocks, the moon, stars, and dreamy lavender clouds like the ones she emerged from during the *Midnights* section of the Eras Tour.

The original album featured thirteen songs, but Taylor later released special editions that had seven more songs. The songs were once again produced by Jack Antonoff and Aaron Dessner. Taylor revealed the track list on the social media app TikTok through a series of videos called Midnights Mayhem with Me. The album embraced elements of electronic pop music, including the use of retro synthesizers from the 1970s. It was nothing like the two eras before it.

This pop album was full of references and callbacks to previous albums and songs. The song "Maroon" is thought to be related to the song "Red," looking back on that same relationship many years later. The song "Question . . . ?" used familiar sounds from the *1989* song "Out of the Woods" and continued the story from the 2014 song. Taylor explained that the album was inspired by the stressful thoughts that keep people up at night.

Songs referenced past relationships, musicians she used to collaborate with, and the man who owned her first six albums at that time, Scooter Braun. The album was about self-confidence and embracing all sides of yourself. It's about being grown-up and looking back on your life and the lessons you've learned. Singles included "Anti-Hero," "Lavender Haze," and "Karma." Taylor also did a couple of duets on the album—"Snow on the Beach" featured singer Lana Del Rey and

Taylor Swift and Ice Spice

a bonus version of "Karma" featured rapper Ice Spice.

Midnights broke a lot of records! It was the highest-streamed album in one day on Spotify. The album spent six weeks at number one on the *Billboard* 200 and was the bestselling album of 2022. Taylor also broke the record for most spots filled in the top ten of the *Billboard* Hot 100, with ten out of the ten spots taken by songs from *Midnights*. She is also the only artist to occupy the entire top five twice. *Midnights* won Album of the Year at the 2022 People's Choice Awards, Favorite Album at the 2023 Kids' Choice Awards, Pop Album of the Year at the iHeartRadio Music Awards, and Album of the Year at the 2023 MTV Video Music Awards. It even won Album of the Year and Best Pop Vocal album at the 2024 Grammys.

Friendship Bracelets!

One of the fan-favorite songs on *Midnights*, "You're on Your Own Kid," started a new fan tradition: trading friendship bracelets! This is thanks to the lyric that talks about making friendship bracelets and living in the moment. When the Eras Tour was announced, Swifties got busy. They bought all the beads that craft stores had all over the country to make these fun accessories. Fans traded bracelets at their shows, walking out with arms full of other Swifties' creations. Some lucky ones even got to trade with Taylor herself or her family and friends.

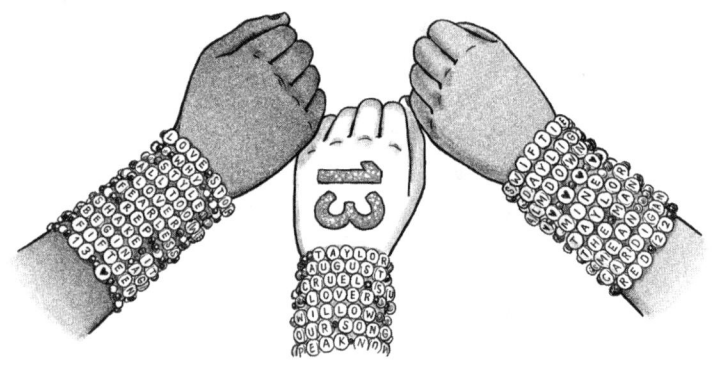

When fans created concert outfits inspired by *Midnights*, they would often wear navy blue with stars or outfits that were covered in sparkling stones like Taylor's costumes in the music video for "Bejeweled."

CHAPTER 11
The *Tortured Poets Department* Era

On February 4, 2024, Taylor attended the Grammy Awards wearing a beautiful draped white gown and a choker with a clock set to midnight.

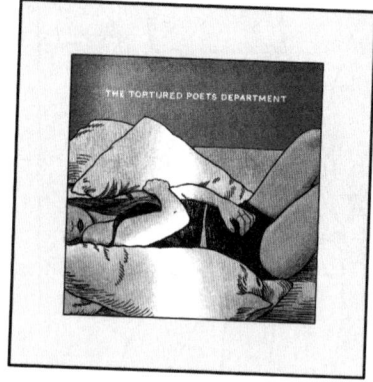

As she accepted the award for Album of the Year for *Midnights*, she surprised everyone by announcing her new album, *The Tortured Poets Department*. She'd been working on the album since 2022, and it spanned the events of her life from the time she completed her previous album, *Midnights*, until then, which meant she'd written it during the Eras Tour.

Taylor described the album as something she needed to write in order to process and get through that busy time in her life. She'd had an overwhelming two years: Her long-term relationship with actor Joe Alwyn ended, she briefly dated musician Matty Healy, and she started a relationship with American football player Travis Kelce. During that time, she was touring the world, releasing "Taylor's Version" albums, directing music videos, and releasing a concert film.

Travis Kelce

It was a hectic time, and Taylor said that writing songs helped her escape from it all.

When the album released on April 19, 2024, Taylor posted on social media that it was an "anthology of new works that reflect events, opinions and sentiments from a fleeting and fatalist moment in time—one that was both sensational and sorrowful in equal measure." What Taylor meant was that the new songs reflected a time in her life that was exciting and fun, but sad and difficult, too.

The white draped gown at the Grammys wasn't the Swifties' first hint into what the cover of this new album might be like. Taylor had been dropping hints for months. She started being photographed in clothes that were themed around literature on her way in and out of the recording studio and out to dinner with friends.

She wore preppy outfits with pleated skirts, loafers, checkered coats, and cozy sweaters. She mixed this academic style with looks inspired by female writers of the past. The colors for this album were called out in the song "The Prophecy" as "shades of greige." By that, Taylor meant somewhere between gray and beige. Popular symbols for the album include typewriters, old-fashioned fountain pens, marble statues, and books.

Florence Welch

The standard edition of the album had sixteen songs on it, including two duets: "Fortnight" (which featured Post Malone) and "Florida!!!" (which featured Florence Welch). Post Malone and Florence

Welch had also helped write these songs.

Lyrically, Taylor wrote about her public and private lives, singing about themes of anger and grief but also humor. Her writing entertained fans in songs like "But Daddy I Love Him."

The album was deeply emotional. Taylor said the songs expressed her "female rage." Musically, this album felt like it drew inspiration from all ten studio albums that came before in terms of sound and genre. It was mostly a synth-pop album, but it also had folk, rock, and country influences that were reminiscent of *folklore*, *reputation*, and *Fearless*. Jack Antonoff and Aaron Dessner produced the album and even cowrote some songs.

The album told the story of a period of Taylor's life when she wasn't taking good care of herself and had some unhealthy habits. Some songs told the story of being in a relationship that seemed great at the time, but looking back she realized it was actually making her life much harder. Other songs were happy, telling the story of a healthy new relationship, as well as about performing on the Eras Tour during a difficult time.

A few hours after *The Tortured Poets Department* released, a second edition of the album, called *The Anthology*, dropped. Fans had been theorizing about the possibility of a double album for months thanks to some hints Taylor had been dropping, like holding up two fingers when accepting her award  and announcing the album, and including the two-fingers emoji in her posts leading up to the release. This double album included the original sixteen songs plus fifteen new bonus songs, for a total of thirty-one. It was the most new songs Taylor had ever released in a single day.

"Fortnight"

The first single of the album, "Fortnight," came with a music video full of beautiful costumes and Easter eggs from past and future eras. In one scene Taylor and Post Malone lie among fluttering papers forming the shape of her side silhouette, an image that is originally from the music video for "Style" from *1989*. There was even a book with "Us" written on the cover, referencing not only her song "The Story of Us" from *Speak Now* but also her collaboration with Gracie Abrams on the song "Us." The typewriter featured in the video is also missing the "1" key—a nod to her song "the 1" on *folklore*. Actors Ethan Hawke and Josh Charles made appearances in the video, a reference to their roles in the film *Dead Poets Society*, which inspired the name of Taylor's album.

The standard-edition cover art featured a black-and-white photo of Taylor in a black outfit lying on a bed, surrounded by a thick white border. Only the bottom half of her face is visible, like the original *1989* cover art. The *Anthology* cover art was different! It featured a black-and-white image of Taylor framed by a black background and a small beige square border.

The Tortured Poets Department became the all-time most-streamed album in a single day (a record that was previously held by Taylor's album *Midnights*), reaching over three hundred million streams. It hit one billion streams in a single week. The album debuted at number one on the *Billboard* 200 chart, and all thirty-one songs from both editions debuted on the *Billboard* Hot 100 list, taking up the first fourteen spots simultaneously. It was the first time that had ever happened in chart history!

billboard HOT 100	
1 Fortnight	Taylor Swift Post Malone
2 Down Bad	Taylor Swift
3 I Can Do It With A Broken Heart	Taylor Swi
4 The Tortured Poets Department	Taylor Sw
5 So Long, London	Taylor Sw
6 My Boy Only Breaks His Favorite Toys	Taylor Swift
7 But Daddy I Love Him	Taylor Swift
8 Floridа!!!	Taylor Swift ft. Florence + the Machine
9 Who's Afraid Of Little Old Me?	Taylor Swift
10 Guilty As Sin?	Taylor Swift
11 Fresh Out the Slammer	Taylor Swift
12 loml	Taylor Swift
13 The Alchemy	Taylor Swift
14 The Smallest Man Who Ever Lived	Taylor Swift

CHAPTER 12
What Era Will Be Next?

There aren't a lot of fans who get to see their favorite artists grow and experiment over the course of their careers the way Taylor Swift's fans have. With the number of songs and albums Taylor has released, there's a song for almost everything one might experience in life, and there's comfort in that. As Taylor has grown as an artist, her fans have grown with her.

As Taylor continues on her journey as a songwriter and performer after the Eras Tour, there will likely be new eras to emerge, with new colors, new songs, and new stories, allowing her style to change while continuing to connect with her fans through her lyrics. But the eras in this book are the ones that she shared with audiences all over the world during the Eras Tour, so they will always be special to those who journeyed far and wide to see their favorite artist celebrate their favorite albums.

On May 30, 2025, Taylor announced that she bought her original masters back for $360 million. This was a huge moment for her, especially after the success of the Taylor's Version albums and the Eras Tour. Taylor felt reunited with the eras that began her career.

Fans across the world will always remember 2023 and 2024 as the years Taylor traveled all over the planet to bring Swifties everywhere the songs that have given them joy, made them feel seen, or simply made them want to dance along with the pop star who dreamed of an exciting life like this when she was just a teenager.

Bibliography

*Books for young readers

Aguirre, Abby. "Taylor Swift on Sexism, Scrutiny, and Standing up for Herself." *Vogue*, August 8, 2019. https://www.vogue.com/article/taylor-swift-cover-september-2019.

*Anderson, Kirsten. *Who Is Taylor Swift?* New York: Penguin Workshop, 2024.

Bernstein, Jonathan. "500 Greatest Albums: Taylor Swift Looks Back on Her 'Only True Breakup Album' 'Red.'" *Rolling Stone*, November 18, 2020. https://www.rollingstone.com/music/music-features/500-greatest-albums-taylor-swift-red-1059586/.

Dickey, Jack. "Taylor Swift on *1989*, Spotify, Her Next Tour and Female Role Models." *Time*, November 13, 2014. https://time.com/3578249/taylor-swift-interview/.

Eells, Josh. "The Reinvention of Taylor Swift." *Rolling Stone*, September 8, 2014. https://www.rollingstone.com/music/music-news/the-reinvention-of-taylor-swift-116925/.

"From McGraw to Midnights: A Retrospective of Taylor Swift's Album Eras and Aesthetics." **ELLE.com**, October 28, 2022. https://www.elle.com/culture/music/a41726787/taylor-swift-all-album-eras-aesthetics-explained/.

Green, Cassandra. "Let Me, a Hardcore Swiftie, Explain the Hidden Meanings in Every One of Taylor Swift's Eras for You." *Marie Claire Australia*. January 23, 2024. https://www.marieclaire.com.au/life/taylor-swift-eras-explained/.

Hiatt, Brian. "Taylor Swift: The Rolling Stone Interview." *Rolling Stone*, September 18, 2019. https://www.rollingstone.com/music/music-features/taylor-swift-rolling-stone-interview-880794/.

*Kaplan, Arie. *96 Facts about Taylor Swift*. New York: Grosset & Dunlap, 2023.

Lansky, Sam. "2023 Person of the Year: Taylor Swift." *Time*, December 6, 2023. https://time.com/6342806/person-of-the-year-2023-taylor-swift/.

Merinuk, Madeline. "Taylor Swift's Eras: What She Was Trying to Say with Each Album's Style." TODAY.com, October 18, 2022. https://www.today.com/popculture/music/taylor-swifts-album-eras-aesthetics-rcna51915.

Wilson, Lana, director. *Miss Americana*. Tremolo Productions, 2020.

Wrench, Sam, director. *Taylor Swift: The Eras Tour*. Taylor Swift Productions, 2023.

YOUR HEADQUARTERS FOR HISTORY

Activities, Mad Libs, and sidesplitting jokes!
Discover the Who HQ books beyond the biographies